ROGER DE GREY

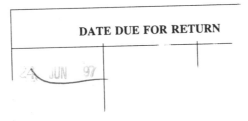
Royal Academy of Arts 11 July – 22 September 1996

First published on the occasion of the exhibition 'Roger de Grey'
Royal Academy of Arts, 11 July–22 September 1996

The production of this catalogue has been made possible
by the generosity of Sir Harry and Lady Djanogly.

Sponsored by and Premiercare

Harpers & Queen and Premiercare are award winners under the
'Pairing Scheme' (National Heritage Arts Sponsorship Scheme)
for their support of the Royal Academy. The Scheme is managed
by the Association for Business Sponsorship of the Arts (ABSA).

The Royal Academy of Arts is grateful to Her Majesty's
Government for its help in agreeing to indemnify the
exhibition under the National Heritage Act 1980, and to the
Museums and Galleries Commission for their help in arranging
this indemnity.

Exhibition Curators: Frank Whitford and Jane Martineau
Exhibition Coordinators: Emeline Max and Susan Thompson
Photographic Coordinator: Miranda Bennion
Editorial Coordinator: Sophie Lawrence

Catalogue design by Hans Schleger & Associates
Printed by Balding + Mansell
Typeset in Joanna by Servis Filmsetting Limited
© 1996 Royal Academy of Arts, London

The curators would like to thank the following for their help:
The Lord Annan; Professor and Mrs Quentin Bell;
The Countess of Bessborough; Judith Bumpus; Cathy Courtney;
Melanie Gardner; Frederick and Connie Gore; Colin Hayes;
Christopher Kingzett; Peter Miall; John Milner; Greville Poke;
Oliver Thomas; Anna Utley

ISBN: 0 900946 4 90

Cover: *Bien Assis* (detail of cat. 54)
Back cover: Roger de Grey working in the studio in Kent

Roger de Grey

Royal Academy of Arts

1996

President's foreword

Roger de Grey was first and foremost a painter. He started painting straight on to the canvas, working out of doors on the Atlantic coast of France or in and around his studio in Kent. Drawing was a separate discipline, and he came to appreciate its virtues later in his career. Structure was central to his vision; the abstract elements of landscape are always present in his paintings; he also appreciated ambiguity, particularly in his *Interior/Exterior* paintings with their half reflections and double shadows.

Secondly Roger de Grey was a teacher, and contributed greatly to the Post-war renaissance of British art schools. From 1947 to 1953 he was tutor at King's College, Newcastle upon Tyne, then part of Durham University, moving to London to work at the Royal College of Art under Robin Darwin, whose influence as an educationalist he always acknowledged and, from 1973 until his death, serving as Principal at the City and Guilds Art School which he brought into the front rank of London art schools. In painting and teaching he worked side-by-side with his wife, the painter Flavia Irwin, whom he first met at the Chelsea School of Art.

At the Academy he is remembered as one of the best-loved and most energetic of Presidents. He served the Academy tirelessly, first from 1976 to 1984 as Treasurer and, from 1984 to 1993, as President, dividing his time between his duties at Burlington House and his teaching at the City and Guilds Art School, but always finding time to paint. His style was apparent in everything he did, from impromptu speeches, to appearing as himself in the staff Christmas pantomime, to his taste for startling viridian socks and ties which he wore with great panache with the President's medal. On his election as President he embarked on planning the new galleries, now named the Sackler Galleries, insisting on the best possible architectural solution to a complex problem. Foster Associates were chosen for the job, and Roger proved to be the ideal client, ceaselessly engaged in the evolution of the project. It is only appropriate that his retrospective exhibition should be held in the galleries that he did so much to create.

We are delighted that *Harpers & Queen* and Premiercare are co-sponsors of this exhibition. This is the fourth show in three years that has benefited from the support of *Harpers & Queen*, and we are particularly pleased to welcome Premiercare as a sponsor at the Academy for the first time.

During his lifetime Roger de Grey never had a retrospective exhibition, but he spoke about it, and had clear views about what such a show should include. As far as was possible the works he himself esteemed have been tracked down and are now on show. The organisers hope that he would have approved of the result. Our thanks go to all those who have lent to the exhibition, many of whom were long-standing friends of Roger's. But our greatest debt is to Flavia Irwin, to Spencer and Robert de Grey and to Emilia Crawford and their families who have given unstintingly of their encouragement, help and counsel. We also thank all those who wrote for the catalogue, the first record of Roger de Grey's art, and to Sir Harry and Lady Djanogly who most generously supported its production. It stands as a memorial to an artist of great distinction.

Sir Philip Dowson CBE
President, Royal Academy of Arts

Roger de Grey

FRANK WHITFORD

The period in which Roger de Grey grew up and became an artist was difficult for English painting. It was dominated by the pretensions of Bloomsbury, fraught with uncertainty, and, with a few exceptions, blighted by insularity.

As a young man de Grey knew little of contemporary foreign art, and, since modernism was not much in evidence in England, he was not an exception. 'You wouldn't believe what the Tate Gallery was like', he later complained, remembering the narrowness of his own and fellow students' horizons. 'That was why we didn't know about 20th-century art. It wasn't there'.[1]

What he did know about was Sickert and the Camden Town Group. Spencer Gore, his mother's brother, was the Group's first President. De Grey inherited his paint-encrusted palette and was surrounded by his work at home. Photographs testify to a striking facial resemblance as well. 'I became a painter', he explained, 'because I was in love with Spencer Gore's painting'.[2]

He never ceased to admire Gore's work − or the rigorously organised and colouristically inventive compositions of his Camden Town associates, Harold Gilman and Charles Ginner. Their traces can clearly be seen in de Grey's first mature paintings.[3]

The young de Grey was proud of the Gore connection not only because of its artistic distinction: Spencer Gore's father was the first singles champion at Wimbledon. The de Greys, who came over with William the Conqueror, had also had their moments. One of them was Archbishop of York. But the life and expectations of Roger de Grey's immediate family seemed wholly conventional, on the surface at least. Their home, a large Georgian house in the Buckinghamshire village of Iver, had several maids, a cook, gardener and nanny in daily attendance and the two sons (Roger was the younger and there was a sister as well) were sent away to school at an early age. But not everything was as comfortable or as conventional as it seemed. Roger's father, Nigel, had no inherited money and budgets were perennially tight. The house was rented and a grandmother took care of the school fees.

Nor was Nigel de Grey an orthodox Edwardian *pater familias*. He married while still a pupil at Eton. Forced to leave the Sixth Form early and unable to go to university, he was obliged to find work wherever he could, in the first instance with the publisher Heinemann.

Nigel de Grey was an amazing man with an immense range of knowledge and the kind of brain which enabled him to complete *The Times* crossword in three minutes flat. He had artistic interests, too. He collected Japanese prints and had a good, if conventional, eye for painting. His uncommon talents, useless in peace time, proved invaluable during the First World War. Recruited into military intelligence, he became a decoder and, in 1916, achieved a remarkable coup by deciphering the Zimmermann Telegram.[4] He worked again in intelligence at Bletchley Park during the Second World War. This gave him welcome respite from the unremarkable career in publishing he had resumed in 1918 − with the Medici Society, the printing of whose reproductions of Old Master paintings he supervised. On one occasion he tried, unsuccessfully, to persuade D.H. Lawrence to write a commentary for children on a selection of Medici reproductions.

Roger de Grey's view of himself as a non-conformist probably owed something to his father's example. But school encouraged a rebellious attitude. Never very healthy, slightly built, sensitive and shy, he was bullied at preparatory school and at Eton.

Preparatory school was St Wilfred's at Seaford, Sussex, which, with its hearty masters, rigorous discipline, and unapologetic philistinism, was entirely typical of its type and time. Noël Annan, two years older than de Grey, remembers the lack of visual stimulus there: 'The only image decorating the walls was an illuminated copy of Kipling's poem If hanging in the dining room'.[5]

But art was part of the curriculum taught by a Miss Burl, a former actress. She made de Grey copy – 'curiously enough, from Medici Christmas cards',[6] an exercise which helped him a great deal. At Eton, where he began to make pastiches of Van Gogh ('painting daffodils with a black line round them'[7]), he learned much more, thanks to the arrival of a new assistant drawing master there.

This was Robin Darwin, a glamorous, ebullient and slightly dis-reputable figure. The great-grandson of Charles Darwin, he was sent down from Cambridge and then left the Slade early after a noisy disagreement with Henry Tonks, the professor. The boys were stunned by the beauty of Darwin's wife, impressed by his vintage yellow Rolls Royce convertible, and intrigued by the drawings of nudes he put up on the walls.

Darwin encouraged de Grey to paint in the open air and introduced him to the cultural excitements of London. Darwin drove him and other boys to the museums and to see the Russian Ballet at Covent Garden. He introduced them to set designers and performers and invited critics to exhibitions of their work. De Grey's career was crucially affected by Robin Darwin, by no means for the last time.

Darwin arranged for him to study at Chelsea Polytechnic, then, thanks to Henry Moore and Graham Sutherland, one of the best art schools in the country. But de Grey had less to do with them than with Robert Medley whose merciless criticism made him doubt his ability and contributed to his growing dissatisfaction with the school.[8]

De Grey later expressed his regret that nothing was compulsory there. Above all he felt the lack of discipline which copying from Old Masters would have imposed. 'I would love to have made transcriptions of Poussin and people', he once admitted. 'I think it was a great loss'. It was 'the new freedom we had been given' which resulted in 'the most inadequate art education' imaginable.[9]

Spencer Gore

Although Flavia Irwin, the fellow student who became his wife, cannot remember de Grey expressing a single criticism of the school, he undoutedly learned most on his own. He became interested in the punctilious realism of the Euston Road painters who opened their school in 1937, the year after he arrived at Chelsea. He admired William Coldstream's sober, tenacious observation of everyday scenes and the similar paintings by Victor Pasmore and Claude Rogers. He felt 'abstract art had reached its climax',[10] and saw in the Euston Road approach a means of revivifying a tired and directionless figurative tradition.

Few art students of any period are happy with their education but de Grey had more reason than most to regret the course of his. In 1939 his studies were interrupted by military service. Serious damage to his left hand – inflicted by a German sniper while he was carrying a wounded man to safety – prevented him from becoming a student again until he was 27 years old.

The War deprived him of those formative years in which, as an artist, he would have been at his most receptive. When he did return to Chelsea towards the end of 1946 the school was more dispiriting than ever. True, he benefited greatly from conversations with Ceri Richards but the studios were so crowded that de Grey often found it impossible to find any space to work. He left after less than a year, most of which had been spent painting in Kent where he lived.

By then he was married, had a young son and was obliged urgently to look for paid employment. Without qualifications, he was lucky to be offered a post teaching at Bedford School. But a chance encounter with Robin Darwin saved him from a dreary career. Not much of a painter himself but blessed with enviable contacts, Darwin had just been appointed Professor of Fine Art at King's College, Newcastle, then part of Durham University. He immediately invited de Grey to join his staff. Inexperienced and artistically unformed, de Grey began work as lecturer in painting in the autumn of 1947.

· · · · · · ·

> I measured away like anything, yes. But. . . I couldn't quite put the little red ticks in, because it seemed to me to be insincere.[11]

At Newcastle de Grey quickly got into his artistic stride. The landscape and figure paintings that he made there are strikingly assured and reveal that concern for tight pictorial structure characteristic of all his later work. The landscapes – of allotments near his home (cat. 1,2) and of Eldon Place, the tree-lined, early 19th-century square in Jesmond, the district where he lived (cat. 3,4, 5) – also demonstrate his ability to endow unpromising, mundane subjects with vitality.

In the allotment paintings, the clearly distinguished planes energised by distinct, stippled marks in pure colour owe something to Bonnard and something to Camden Town, but the portraits and life paintings show that his interest in the Euston Road School had now become dominant. The obvious studio setting and pose of *Interior, Newcastle* (cat.10), the subtle tonal shifts between the figure and ground, and the clear sense of precisely measured formal relationships owe everything to the example of Euston Road.

This is not surprising. There were so many connections between Newcastle and the Euston Road that it looked as though there had been a takeover. Coldstream and Claude Rogers were external examiners, and Lawrence Gowing, Coldstream's most successful pupil, succeeded Darwin as professor in 1948. Victor Pasmore, too, was on the staff – although he, to general dismay, had left his earlier principles behind and was fast abandoning figuration entirely. Gowing was precisely de

Roger de Grey's wartime identity card

Grey's age, but his formidable knowledge lent him an authority beyond his years which a pronounced stutter, gawky appearance and donnish manner did nothing to minimise.

'Suddenly this extraordinary character appeared . . . who was both the most well educated and most literate and articulate man I've ever met, and a total sort of barbarian. . . .'[12] Gowing recognised a kindred spirit in the less assured de Grey, admired his painting and helped him find a London dealer.

Both were 'trying to discover. . .some new attitude to figurative art',[13] which would serve as a sheet anchor in an ocean of stylistic turbulence. But de Grey, even at his most indebted to the Euston Road School, was conscious that relentless measuring was essentially illogical, informed less by intuition than theory. The obtrusive reference points, always left visible on the finished canvas, also seemed mannered, and redundant.

For a time de Grey dotted and carried, too, painstakingly mapping his way across the surfaces of his motifs. But although some traces of measuring remain he usually covered them up entirely. Figure painting was not de Grey's strength in any case. He found landscape more congenial and he now concentrated on a small number of motifs, among them Eldon Place and other views which included geometric elements like gasometers and factory chimneys (cat. 13).

He used a precisely modulated, limited range of colour and directional brushstrokes grouped into blocks to suggest form, structure and spatial progression. He introduced framing arrangements of trees in the middle distance and high horizon lines to emphasise the picture plane. These devices recall Cézanne. Like him, de Grey now aspired to a kind of painting charged with tension and ambiguity. Spatial illusion, although vital, was to be countered throughout the canvas by the assertive identity of the paint itself.

Thanks to both Cézanne and the Euston Road, de Grey came to understand the complexity of seeing and the importance of artificial conventions in the recording of visual experience. He may still have believed that abstraction had run its course but was now paradoxically thinking more and more like an abstract painter. He became especially intrigued by a pictorial problem which would be crucial for his ideas about painting. Since space can be both continuous and compartmentalised, how can a series of distinct but related spaces – for example the interior of a room together with the view through its windows – be united into a coherent and convincing whole?

De Grey repeatedly addressed the problem in a magisterial series of paintings made at various moments throughout his career. The first dates from the Newcastle period. Called *The Open Window* (p. 22), it showed his wife repairing a sheet at a window overlooking Eldon Place. A vertical window frame both separated and pictorially integrated the interior and exterior spaces. Given the importance of similar subjects for de Grey's later work, it is a pity that *The Open Window* no longer exists. Dissatisfied with the figure, de Grey cut the canvas in two.

· · · · · · ·

I think I may have painted some quite good pictures at the time, but I think I was disturbed by what was going on. . ... I couldn't quite relate my work to what was happening. . . .[14]

At Newcastle, de Grey, reacting against the liberalism from which he believed he had suffered at Chelsea, introduced specific tasks and exercises designed to impose discipline. He devised ways of presenting familiar objects in unexpected contexts or arrangements so as to help students to see them as if for the first time. The aim was a kind of drawing free from unthinking reliance on easy, derivative mannerisms.

At the end of 1953 de Grey became Senior Tutor in painting at the Royal College of Art. By then Robin Darwin had become Rector of the RCA, and was so anxious to have his former pupil and colleague on the staff that he gave him no more than three hours to accept his invitation. The discipline de Grey had imposed at undergraduate level at Newcastle was unwelcome at the College. All the students there were graduates who, in theory at least, already knew precisely what they were doing and why they were doing it. Most bridled at interference from teachers to whom they gave respect only when they thought they had earned it.

By then de Grey enjoyed a modest but growing reputation as a painter. His work had been shown at galleries in London, and in 1949 he had won a prize at the Carnegie International Exhibition in Pittsburgh. His work had also been noticed by several critics. An anonymous review of a mixed show in *The Times* for 7 February 1950, for example, observed that, of his fellow exhibitors (who included Robin Darwin), Roger de Grey had 'the boldest and most original talent. . . . He is also an excellent colourist, limited in range but at the same time markedly individual'.

The title of Senior Tutor sounded grand but it involved heavy responsibilities. The Professor of Painting, Rodrigo Moynihan, came and went more or less as he pleased while de Grey was expected to be always available, taking the brunt of the teaching and paper work. Teaching was difficult. True, some of the most distinguished British painters of the day, including Carel Weight and Ceri Richards, were on the staff, but their interests seemed diametrically opposed to those of their most able students.

Yet, looking back on it, the painting department at the Royal College was then more lively and productive than at any time before or since. Sensitive to each successive innovation, trend and fashion, and originating several of its own, the department produced the 'kitchen sink' style and then succumbed to the dangerous attractions of American Abstract Expressionism before inventing several varieties of Pop Art. These propelled the RCA into the international spotlight and made several students media celebrities. Their commercial success added to the difficulty of teaching them.

De Grey was alarmed at the course the art world was taking. He felt marginalised. He realised that he knew less about some kinds of contemporary painting, especially American, than many of his students. According to him, the teachers 'always seemed to be one pace behind. The students knew through magazines what was happening in America, and we used to spend hours discussing their work and questioning all our values. It was difficult to break away and think about yourself as a painter.'[15]

Robin Darwin

It was also difficult, given the liberal and eclectic atmosphere (Mark Rothko, visiting the College, was distressed to find abstract and figurative painters working side-by-side in the same studios), to persuade students to undertake exercises of any kind: 'I set up a very elaborate room of plaster casts and mirrors and reflected light . . . which I thought was going to transform the art of painting into something quite new, but I don't think it did'.[16]

Never the less, some students saw the point of the discipline. One of them was David Hockney who once recalled that de Grey and his other teachers 'left you fairly free, as long as you did drawing, because in those days that was still compulsory – which was fine with me. . . .'[17]

Of equal importance were the group tutorials which de Grey insisted on, and which worked well. 'When you got Leonard Rosoman and Sandra Blow and Robert Buhler and one or two others together, and we saw . . . sometimes more than one student at a time, it became quite an interesting discussion . . . as to the sort of directions that art was taking at that time. . . .'[18]

However helpful such talk might have been to the students it did little to bolster de Grey's confidence in his own work. It was, as he said, 'difficult to maintain one's sense of identity',[19] and some characteristics of the paintings he produced during the mid-1960s suggest something close to a crisis. In works like *The Garden Opposite* (cat. 27), for example, the motif becomes difficult to read in some places, the blocks of colour are needlessly assertive, and the pronounced curves and other structural

Voting during the Painting School entrance examination at the Royal College of Art in 1966. l-r: Peter Blake, Leonard Rosoman, Roger de Grey, Carel Weight, Jean Cook

devices are so obtrusive as to look mannered. In *Little Buckland I* (cat. 28) looser, more expressive passages dominate still more and suggest that de Grey was concentrating less on the motif than the abstract, painterly effects it suggested.

The uncertainty such compositions betray did not afflict him for long, however. De Grey came to terms with his doubts and, challenged by the eclectic styles of his students, returned to the close scrutiny and transcription of nature. This did not mean a slavish subservience to the motif but a fine balance between the observed and the constructed. Structure and pattern, clear in all his work, now became more obvious – nowhere more so than in the series of paintings called *Interior/Exterior*. Most of them were made in de Grey's studio, a converted cowshed with windows extending from floor to ceiling on both sides. The studio is set apart from his home in Kent. An orchard is on one side, a meadow on the other, and the large windows on one side disclose a view of a small walled garden surrounded by trees. De Grey used the studio windows in various permutations as framing devices within each painting so as to capture that contradictory feeling of separateness from, yet unity with, nature he always experienced there.

One of the most daring works in the series is an *Interior/Exterior* of 1977 (cat.32), owned by the Tate Gallery. The window frame echoes the edges of the canvas, itself a pronounced vertical, so as to create an arrangement of three rectangles which both fragment and unify the view. The dominant geometry of the window contrasts with the organic forms of the trees to create a satisfying visual dynamic. The geometry also reminds us that the picture is not just – or even principally – an illusion. It is also an object in its own right with its own distinct physical characteristics.

This painting was executed entirely in the studio, where even compositions begun out-of-doors were almost always finished. Only away from the motif and its confusing complexity could de Grey achieve the clear structural schemes he perceived in nature: 'I used to believe that you had to begin and finish a painting in front of the motif. But . . . I can't do that any more. . . . I have to bring the paintings back and work for a very long time on them, and somehow they begin to change for all sorts of different reasons that I can't really explain . . . except that one mark makes one think of another and it perceptively alters the nature of the painting.'[20]

For de Grey, then, a painting inspired by nature was far more than a literal transcription of it. Paradoxically, he captured the essence of the motif most convincingly when he could no longer see it. An image resembling the motif had to emerge during the process of mark making. He always knew that copying nature is an impossibility: 'Painting what you see is in itself an abstraction . . . there's no such thing as copying because there's no way you can copy a space, a mood, an atmosphere. What you put down is an interpretation of what you see. . . .'[21]

• • • • • • •

An obsession for working out-of-doors has been the motivation and the limitation of my painting.[22]

When de Grey resigned from the Royal College in 1973 it was not the place he had joined twenty years before. It now had new buildings (although not for the painters), university status – and the pretensions that went with it – and many new faces.

One of them belonged to Lord Esher (Lionel Brett), an architect and another Old Etonian, who succeeded Robin Darwin as Rector in 1971. Darwin cast a long and intimidating shadow, but Esher's toughest task was dealing not with the past but the present, increasingly politicised by disaffected students and dissatisfied staff unions. The RCA was spared the kind of disruption which afflicted other art schools in Britain, Hornsey above all, but it suffered much more from a sour and rancorous atmosphere.

When de Grey left the RCA there was nothing waiting for him elsewhere, and this is a measure of the strength of his feelings about an institution he had served for two decades. But he did not have to wait long for another appointment. Before the year was out he became Principal of the City and Guilds of London School at Kennington.

That School was beset with problems of a different kind. It was small (with 175 students) and had huge financial difficulties. Recently made independent of the City and Guilds Institute and ill-equipped to fend for itself, it suffered a further blow when the Inner London Education Authority was dissolved and Lambeth, its local borough, refused to support the school.

Largely because of de Grey's talent as a fund-raiser, the school was not only saved but managed to expand. Adjacent buildings were acquired and new courses – in wood carving, stone carving, lettering and the decorative arts – introduced. The school underwent a renaissance, not least because it offered a mixture of craft, fine and applied art that could be found in no other institution. It also insisted on compulsory life drawing.

As if he were not busy enough at Kennington, de Grey was at the same time heavily involved with the Royal Academy. His association with the Academy was by then long and distinguished. He had first shown a painting at the Summer Exhibition of 1947, and from 1956 his work was an almost annual feature of the show. In 1962 he was elected an Associate and became a full Academician seven years later. In 1975 he was appointed to the Exhibitions Committee and in 1976 was made Treasurer.

In these two posts he demonstrated a rare gift for administration and financial management, and it was this, together with his popularity among his fellow Academicians, which ensured that he was elected – with an overwhelming majority on the first ballot – President in December 1984.

This is not the place to rehearse de Grey's singular achievements as PRA. But something must be said about his quietly reformist activities which he once revealingly described as the result of 'perfectly proper subversion'.[23] The Sackler Galleries were planned and built; Summer Exhibitions were enlivened by contributions from invited artists; the category Associate of the Royal Academy was abolished; the membership was broadened to embrace many of those who previously wanted nothing to do with an institution which they regarded as reactionary; the exhibitions programme became one of the most ambitious and exciting in Europe.

Given de Grey's responsibilities at Burlington House and the City and Guilds School it is difficult to understand how he found the time to paint. But he did more than that. The work of the final decade was better than ever.

His art remained the centre of his life. He reserved several days a week for it in term-time and more during vacations. In term, most of the painting was done in the Kent studio while in vacations he worked at his house in France, in the Charente-Maritime.

The area around his French home with its woods, rivers, and salt marshes stretching away across a plain towards the Atlantic inspired some of his most magnificent paintings. In works like *Marennes* (cat. 51) de Grey addressed and triumphantly solved intimidating pictorial problems. The giddyingly high viewpoint, lack of a strong foreground element and dominant middle distance are not allowed to compromise the tonal, colouristic and spatial unity or the vivid impression of heat, haze and unquantifiable distance.

Yet he nowhere attempted to disguise the means with which he achieved the illusion. Directional brushmarks, passages of scumbled paint and, especially in the foreground, spatters and other seemingly accidental marks – some applied with lengths of wood and the fingers – assert their own identity without destroying the illusion. The same is true of the major compositional elements. The curving road in the foreground, the layered narrow horizontal bands of the fields and the verticals of the poplars close to the horizon are descriptive of reality without losing their character as independent forms. Here, more clearly than ever, we can sense the fluidity of the boundary in de Grey's work between figuration and abstraction.

De Grey once described himself as 'a very limited painter': 'You come to terms with what you can do. There are all sorts of imaginative areas I cannot enter'.[24] The modesty was typical of the man, and modesty together with a constant awareness of the gulf between his ambition and achievement hindered his progress as a painter. A horror of whatever seemed meretricious or insincere did the same. He had other difficulties to cope with, too, most obviously the constant, clamorous demands of teaching and administration.

Yet somehow he transcended them all to make an enduring contribution to British art. In characteristically self-deprecating fashion de Grey often said that he wished he could have been an abstract painter but lacked the necessary imagination. But he must have known that the power of his work derives precisely from the seductive way it draws attention to its own essentially abstract nature.

This article is especially indebted to information contained in Andrew Lambirth's interview with Roger de Grey. It was recorded between 20 September and 15 December 1994 for the British Library National Sound Archive where the tapes and a transcript are preserved. References to the transcript are given here simply as 'Lambirth'.

[1]Interview with Lucy Hughes-Hallet, ES Magazine (supplement to The Evening Standard), 3 December 1993, p. 8.
[2]Lambirth, p. 20.
[3]This enthusiasm produced some startling pronouncements. Talking about the fine colour sense of the Camden Town painters, de Grey once described Monet as 'a vulgarian ... in comparison with his English counterparts. I mean Gilman had the most marvellous sense of colour that it's possible to imagine ... these dense, close-toned colours which are simply unequalled anywhere'. Lambirth, pp. 23–4.
[4]Arthur Zimmermann, the German foreign minister, sent a coded telegram to the Japanese and Mexican governments, urging them to attack the United States and promising support. When the British informed the US of this they declared war against Germany and its allies, altering the course of the conflict.
[5]Conversation with the author, 14 December 1995.
[6]Lambirth, pp. 10–11.
[7]Lambirth, p. 20.
[8]De Grey later came to understand Medley's methods and admitted that he, too, 'was cruel when (he) first started teaching', because 'when you're young ... you think you've got something to teach'. Lambirth, p. 29.
[9]Lambirth, p. 45.
[10]Quoted after Paddy Kitchen, 'Coming to Terms, Roger de Grey, PRA', Country Life, May 29 1986, p. 1540.
[11]Lambirth, p. 50.
[12]Lambirth, p. 61.
[13]Lambirth, p. 62.
[14]Lambirth, p. 83.
[15]ibid.
[16]Lambirth, p. 65.
[17]Christopher Frayling, The Royal College of Art, One Hundred and Fifty Years of Art and Design, London, 1987, p. 162.
[18]Lambirth, pp. 82-3.
[19]Lambirth, p. 83.
[20]Recorded conversation with the author in the series 'Artists and the Landscape', broadcast on Radio 3 on 21 February 1994, produced and edited by Judith Bumpus.
[21]ibid.
[22]Quoted from an obituary in The Times, 16 February 1995.
[23]Interview with Charles Darwent, in 'A Country Portrait', Country Homes and Interiors, July 1991, p. 116.
[24]Kitchen, p. 1540.

Roger de Grey : Painter

It was to painting (his own and everyone else's) that Roger dedicated his working life. His extraordinary gifts as a leader were wholly tied to the strength of character, patience, optimism and intelligence with which he honed his skill as an artist. Turning over my earliest memories, I suddenly recalled something at the de Greys that was very important – a christening. Now I realise it must have been Roger's. In spite of this closeness in childhood, I don't think we ever talked much about painting, largely because we sensed we were in agreement. The influence of his uncle, Spencer Gore, on both of us has been rather overstated. The truth is that continually living with his work as children, and because the tradition in which he worked was so central to the course of Impressionism and Post-Impressionism, we were quite naturally heirs to the whole corpus of late 19th-century and early 20th-century French painting. Our problem was what to select and where to try and take it. Roger once mentioned his irritation that at Chelsea Art School, while he was struggling to find a good way to paint from the model, Ceri Richards had asked why didn't he try painting like Harold Gilman (Spencer Gore's close colleague). Roger had to distance himself from Camden Town. It was clear that he was not going to throw away what he had gained from his heritage, but within this canon he was determined to break new ground.

His very earliest schoolboy promise had been as a happy-go-lucky Impressionist: bright broken colour and loose dabs of paint. After the War his mother, shocked at the severity of the discipline which he was imposing on himself, expressed a fear that perhaps the change was due to what he had suffered in his tank during the War. I still think it more likely that the maturity found in the War gave him the power to resist the expectations of family and friends as to what sort of artist he was going to be and to follow a course which meant deliberate choice and conscious effort. The choice of Cézanne as a master now seems to have been inevitable. It would be approved by his colleagues at Newcastle who had been associated with the Euston Road School, Lawrence Gowing or Victor Pasmore. Cézanne was also, even if accidentally, the father of abstract painting. The discussion raised by Victor Pasmore's conversion to pure abstraction enthused all of us who believed in a developing modern movement. Roger has throughout shown his sympathy for a fully figurative and descriptive naturalism and equally for complete abstraction. His work is a compelling synthesis of these apparently completely opposed tenancies in which neither is fudged nor diminished.

I think of a painting he showed in the 1970s: trees on each side of a mountain path. The play of light on the movement of foliage is translated into small flat facets quite disjointed from the background, which swing like little bits of paper in a curve over the path. I see why he admired Vieira da Silva so much. In several paintings of the 1980s, Ile d'Oléron or La Tremblade, lines, even double lines indicating ditches, banks, walls or pathways between waterways and water meadows form strong abstract grids cutting through the painting, while in between little scribbles of paint nestle as if something out of Twombly's world. Quite clearly here are two different kinds of abstract symbol, but the painting still breathes the secret poetry of the place. He found, and constructed, his own unconventional subject-matter. What of the studio with big windows to the floor that he built to make his very own indoor–outdoor world, in a wooded corner between an orchard and Camer park? Here he could smell the Kentish air and mix a still-life into the landscape; partly with tender affection for the setting, partly as a puritanical essay in parallel verticals. There he also painted himself at work.

Roger made sure that he had his time to paint. One reason for eventually finding a house in France was to provide a haven away from the inescapable obligations of London. Both Flavia and Roger found wonderful material there. Roger, during this last decade, treated water and earth, foliage and sky more lavishly in paint, richer in colour, responding to the seasons and the essential character and poetry of each separate view. What is quite rare nowadays is the strength he had to go on working on a painting until it really was finished. In doing so he not only increased sensual pleasure from the landscape but also from the gradually evenly all-over built up surface of the paint – that strangely realistic substitute for the texture of the world.

The duality in his painting hinges on the realisation that nature cannot be copied: the search is for an appropriate symbolic language in which it can be discussed. Nobody today has made a more thorough or disciplined research into what we see and how to represent it. So it is no surprise that during his Presidency a symposium was held together with the Royal Society of Medicine on visual perception, with contributions from a psychologist, a doctor, a philosopher, an artist, even a theorist on virtual reality.

Recently it was agreed that a composite picture (or rather a series of pictures) is built up from reactions to visual stimuli in disparate parts of the brain. We are unconscious of how these pictures are composed; they simply appear as the reality of the world in which we live. In fact, they are a description of the external world in a code which is conditioned by the physical structure of our brains, eyes, nervous systems. The history of art is also a history of how we see, often parallel to science. Where psychologists in this field were always loth to accept that our minds could construct a realistic vision without conscious knowledge, artists – training themselves to isolate tone, colour, line, planes, solids, space, perspectives, patterns, textures, each as separable functions – have always known pretty well that they were detailing consciously, as it were in very slow motion, the functions which eye and brain perform without our knowledge.

The landscape painter is always close to that primary sensation of seeing, and therefore the mystery of our existence. It is because of the ties between the work of painters of Roger's enquiring kind with such current ideas in physical science and semiology, as well as the consciousness that what happens to the land and the oceans really matters, which leaves me to see Roger's work as reaching towards the future and therefore enduring.

Frederick Gore and Roger de Grey at the Annual Press
Conference, Royal Academy, January 1985

Walking down Exhibition Road we might agree that painting
had taken on board too many socio-political and pseudo-philosophical
ideas. The descriptive element should have an assured simplicity in
describing truly the character of a head or the mood of a landscape, the
abstract element, tentative and yet mathematical, of composition and
colour might, if one was lucky, speak of profounder things by tuning
into universal harmonies and discords. But mostly what we discussed
was technical. The meaning of a painting starts with the way it is
painted. He once remarked (curiously in referring to his landscapes and
still-lifes in which the whole of a canvas is so faithfully covered and the
parts so interrelated) that he knew he was in trouble when he found he
was working all over a canvas at once. I suppose he felt that he had to
establish some centre or centres in the canvas to set the pace and mood
of the whole. Every painting was an experiment.

He said some very interesting things in a broadcast interview on
Radio 3 in February 1994 in answer to the question 'do you paint what
you see?' He made the point that painting what you see is in itself an
abstraction: you cannot copy but must interpret what you see. For
Roger evidently, as for Cézanne, there is a conflict to be resolved
between the demands of painting (the language the painter must use)
and the objects which he sees, which, after all, have inspired him to
start the painting. Of course we only know the real world from ideas
from all sorts of sources with which we test our experience of it.
Nevertheless, for the realist it is not possible to ignore the appearance of
things. Thus he says 'I am curiously obsessed by reality in a sort of way
I can't explain to you, but it does obtrude and often destroy what I do'.

He was not interested in the changing light effects of sunset and
sunrise. 'I am not out and about at sunset, I'm having a drink, and I
don't get up very early in the morning'. He does paint out-of-doors. He
follows those Impressionists who started without a preparatory drawing
straight on to the canvas. But starting as a painter who believed that he
must finish a painting on the spot, he eventually finds that he must
spend more and more time developing, strengthening and refining
indoors what he is seeking in the landscape. The painting develops its
own life. The image is born in the imagination. He has left Impressionism
behind.

'Almost always I start painting and turn my back on it and paint in
some other direction. It's quite strange that always I've got the feeling
that something more extraordinary is behind me or just to one side if I
could move a fraction'. Essentially he is out to contradict the idea that a
painting of objects and the conditions in which they exist is like a view
through a window or a stage set. He says 'I paint right in the middle of
the motive'. The spectator must be put where the artist is: inside the
canvas and in space. He resists the temptation offered by Cubism, or the
cinematographic montage of the 1920s, to scramble a number of
different viewpoints or images into one composition. To be truthful in
still-life, portraiture and landscape especially, a canvas must have a
coherent manageable organisation and virtually a single theme
responding to intellect, visual sensation and emotion. But we can see

that he permits himself experimental perspectives, a tilted, almost vertical ground plane and structural ambiguities, also arbitrary changes of scale, coaxing the whole painting into a very beguiling unity.

Roger's painting is surely about the nature of visual perception and thus dedicated to an acute and passionate observation of a chosen natural environment. But it is also an exploration of the painter's language. The fact that the basic signs (*signifiers*) in this looser visual system of communication are heavily *motivated* (look like the things they represent) while the signifiers in a verbal system are more obviously *arbitrary* does not mean that these basic signs are any less abstract. There are no lines visible in nature: linearity is set in the mental activity by which we recognise objects. Pigments bear a tenuous relationship to the colours which we see constantly changing with the light; Canvas is flat: the literal imitation of shadows and shading destroys the very volumes which 'tone' is supposed to represent. The painter's task must be with these abstract means of lines and shapes and colours to interpret the landscape and to share his discoveries with us.

But painting is also experimental. For Roger the experiment starts with the physical process by which the painting is made. In his Reynold's Lecture (1986) on the derivations of modernism the most eloquent passages are apropos Picasso, Monet and Cézanne. 'The rejection of the preconceived subject, now the subject was no longer the subject, in favour of its attributes of space, light and atmosphere, implied that the organisation of surface had to be drawn from the morning air and invented from the first paint marks to appear on the canvas in response to the impulse unfolded afresh in every glance.' Enthralled by the direct use of colour on a white canvas he sides with his uncle Spencer Gore who followed Camille Pissarro's example. He dismisses Sickert: 'for colour layers mixed, judged, assessed, and then applied to a predetermined tonal plan, reviewed against the warm earth or cool greenish tint of the undercoat, were very different to a pure colour chosen on impulse for its relevance to a received sensation after a single act of observation, dabbed in a short stroke onto the white surface, applied again to enlarge the quantity, but instantly transformed by the next reference to the motif. This reference would confirm that no single colour can represent the translucency, the sparkle, the density of the shadow cast on the gravelled road at the entry to the village. Is this then the new way of imitating nature?' This accompanied a slide of Pissarro's *The Crossroads, Pontoise* that led on to the Fauves and Matisse, the instantaneous directness of the later Picasso.

Paintings such as *Broue* or *Marennes* seem to me to be masterpieces of faithful and imaginative representation, but with extraordinary compositional devices, such as the shadow of the bridge, itself scarcely visible in the painting, striding across the canvas.

This was Roger's own description of that countryside: 'It's painted in a sort of heat haze. This is a tremendously hot part of France. The landscape is perfectly flat as far as you can see and right in the distance there is the sea. This used to be sea and it was reclaimed in the Middle Ages and there's just this great escarpment with a castle at the top and you stand there and the whole panorama is laid out like a carpet in front of you. The really original part of one's work comes out of some sort of observable thing that happens in a week, in a day, in a minute and I think its much more important than what the painting looks like. What the painting looks like is almost beyond your control because what you see, what you come to understand about what you're looking at, is more important in the formation of the painting than a conscious desire to make it look like one thing or another.'

'I would like', he says, 'to have been an abstract painter. Abstract painting fascinates me from the sheer imaginative invention of it. You can't believe that people can be so inventive. And I would like to have been that sort of person. You just have to accept that you are who you are...'. Here he is hardly fair to himself – the point being that he could quite easily have been an abstract painter if he could have abandoned the joys of observation in a universe – which is *per se* more inventive than man can be – for a form of painting relying on the harmony and discords of relationships of colour and mathematics of form. His reply to the last question, 'What does the landscape, nature, mean to you?' suggests that the sacrifice would have been too great: 'I get so excited by achieving effects. The world we inherit is such a glittering marvel that occasionally you just achieve, perhaps not by looking at it or anything else, but by closing your eyes and making a stab, you achieve something of the glitter and the play of the way the forms work in relation to each other, the juxtaposition of forms and suddenly one part of it is lit'.

Roger de Grey in his studio

Quotations on pp. 17–19 are taken from a recorded conversation between Roger de Grey and Frank Whitford in the series *Artists and Landscape* broadcast on Radio 3 on 21 February 1994, produced and edited by Judith Bumpus. Roger de Grey's Reynolds Lecture, *Route Verte to Twentieth-Century Painting*, delivered at the Royal Academy on 6 February 1986, was published the same year.

Eton and Chelsea

OLIVER THOMAS

Roger de Grey,
Portrait of Oliver Thomas,
c. 1937, Private Collection

Oliver Thomas,
Portrait of Roger de Grey,
c. 1937, Private Collection

At the opening of the Mantegna exhibition I heard Roger tell how the mauve colour of the walls was arrived at by mixing colours in his Aunt May's watercolour box. This took me back to when I was thirteen and Roger fourteen; I sat in his room at Eton while he painted little plain wooden boxes in some form of opaque watercolour. Each colour he mixed pleased him more than the last, each facet would be a different colour. That's my very first memory of Roger painting; delicacy and refinement, anything but clumsiness. I cannot remember the first picture I knew. An early one was a self-portrait embodying the word ENO'S in red (he was fond of Eno's at the time). Not coming from an artistic family but beginning to be drawn towards some change of attitude, I felt this picture might be the inception of a new movement. Roger pronounced it to be bad and destroyed it.

I found in my studio recently a painting on plywood which Roger must have done when he was just sixteen. This painting of a Mediterranean harbour – not uninfluenced by Robin Darwin, our art teacher – was produced in an afternoon and was one in a series. It smacks of scene-painting. Indeed, Roger painted scenery as well as being the producer of marionette-stage productions which Robin Darwin had us all doing in the Eton Drawing Schools. Roger loved the stage, partly through his uncle Spencer Gore's paintings of the music hall, partly through family participation in the Canterbury Old Stagers and partly through the influence of Sickert on him as on Spencer Gore. Exhibited at the Royal Academy in 1949 was his painting of Ralph Alderson as Sir Peter Teazle in *The Rivals*. In the vast chapel at Eton on a holy day when the *Gloria* was sung in Latin I caught Roger's eye through the crowd of heads as we sang '*sicut erat in principo...*'. 'How did you translate that?' I asked him. 'Sickert was very much in evidence'.

While Roger was still in his teens at Eton he produced a series of pictures during a summer holiday at Little Gaddesden. These pictures on coarse canvas impressed me greatly. They had the characteristic, which Roger kept through his life, of great impact. There was one with the curving branches of a fir-tree in the foreground rather as in some of Cézanne's paintings of *Montagne St Victoire*.

When we went to Chelsea Art School we resolved to draw from life. The life class was dominated by Heroys – a general in the pre-revolutionary Russian army. Roger's need to learn to draw was far less desperate than mine, so I don't think he altogether liked the brisk teaching method of Heroys. With a very black pencil, with the lead held from flying away by his thumb pressed down on it, he would say 'Arshitectoor, moor arshitectoor', and then starting a standing pose at the ball of the foot, his pencil shot up over the top of one's hesitant drawing. Harold Williamson's remarkable staff at Chelsea also included Moore, Sutherland and Robert Medley, who was to have the most influence on Roger.

Many an afternoon Roger and I went round the galleries. Sickert was still much in evidence, while paintings by Cézanne and Pissarro were for sale, also Derain's London paintings. In the New Burlington Galleries we saw *Guernica* and all its terrifying associated drawings. A three-man show – Bonnard, Braque and Picasso – stands out in my memory. It was Bonnard who stirred Roger most deeply, while the paintings of Braque continued to affect the paint surface of his paintings and kept him striving towards abstraction even as he shunned it.

Students at Chelsea were very varied in age and background. Individually, I remember George Haslam, highly intelligent, deeply interested in music, film and later, television; he was aware of Roger's talent. Paul Miller was a beautiful draughtsman; and there was Flavia Irwin whom we both adored, and Roger loved and married. I remember her dust-cover for *Where Angels Fear to Tread*; I remember drawings and a painting of trees bent by sea-winds.

In the spring and early summer of 1939 Roger and I painted near Yeovil. His cousin Violet Clive, a widow, lived at Brympton. Usually we painted apart on different motifs, though I recall painting at Odcombe where Roger was just up the hill behind me and our motifs were the same. Curiously, his picture seemed to indicate that he was closer than me to the foreground hedge, though in fact he was further away. Our paintings were done in the open air and seldom exceeded two foot by three. I remember my own work but Roger's far less clearly. In his paintings all the elements come onto the surface of the picture. He avoided illusionism as do Cézanne or Bonnard. There is a portrait sketch of me and another of him by me painted within one day in the oasthouse studio at Plaxtol, each of us painted for half an hour and each sat for half an hour. I doubt if either of us had more than three half-hour turns.

The war came very soon after Somerset, and each of us went to different parts of the army. During a coinciding leave I met Roger and Flavia in Oxford. Flavia told me to go to the gardens of Worcester College. Later, during captivity in the Far East, I used to think of them, and when I returned home in November 1945 I succeeded in getting a place at Worcester. This didn't cut me off from Roger and Flavia. They lived at Eynsham so that Roger could get treatment for a wounded hand at the Wingfield. He had done a number of topographical drawings. He gave me one of Trinity, Oxford, in pen and ink, conté and wash – rather romantic, reflecting something of the mood of those of us who had, slightly to our own surprise, survived the War. He was not long at Eynsham and returned very soon to Chelsea.

In the autumn of 1946 I painted a picture of the canal at Oxford as it passes close under the boundary wall of Worcester College. In 1947 I submitted it to the Academy, and went along on non-members' Varnishing Day to take a furtive look. As I was about to enter out came Roger. 'Well, we've stormed the portals', he said. We walked round together. Roger's *At the Sink*, a rather low-toned Camden-Townish painting, was on the line, my *Canal and River, Oxford* was not. It seemed immensely high and to have grown very small.

Roger de Grey,
Ralph Alderson as Sir Peter Teazle
exhibited at the Academy in the
Summer Exhibition, 1949

Newcastle

RALPH HOLLAND

In the autumn of 1950 I found myself taking up a post as a lecturer in the Newcastle division of the University of Durham. The head of my department was the clever and exuberant Lawrence Gowing. The department taught painting, sculpture, fabric and stained-glass design and the history of art – my responsibility.

I must have already met Roger de Grey at my interview, after which Professor Gowing had presided over a tea for the staff. I was impressed by Lawrence, by a good Dutch 17th-century portrait on his wall and by the appearance of tea in a massive silver service. The atmosphere was that of a minor and unfashionable Oxbridge college. It was only later I discovered that the tea service had been borrowed by Roger, on Lawrence's instructions, from a local shop.

Though both of us were extremely busy, through the kindness of Roger and his wife, Flavia, I slipped into a friendship particularly welcome to a bachelor parted from London friends. The de Greys lived in Eldon Place, a delightful and unexpected cul-de-sac, in an irregular early 19th-century terrace of houses facing onto gardens, trees and, on the opposite side of the narrow road, more trees and the back of the University library. At one end of the terrace a tablet on the wall recorded the fact that the house had been lived in by George Stephenson. Eldon Place was to provide an important source of motifs for paintings, as later were the fields and woods round the house in Meopham.

Inside, the Eldon Place house was comfortably untidy and made enviable by pieces of old furniture, mostly acquired in the local sale room; a mid-Georgian tallboy, a late 18th-century French desk and interesting small decorative objects which the younger children were liable to throw out of the window into the garden; Emilia, an energetic baby uncertainly confined in a play pen; Robert not yet at school and Spencer, the oldest child, who later as an architect was to help create the Sackler Galleries at Burlington House.

One turns over old memories like fading snapshots; touring the Newcastle junk shops with Roger; a freezing day sitting with the children on the coal-strewn beach at Whitley Bay which Roger claimed to enjoy; Roger painting his wife seated sewing by a window in the drawing room at Eldon Place; being driven to Seaton Delaval when the car's necessarily frugal supply of petrol ran out in open country. Other snapshots record Roger's equanimity on being confronted by a scene of Hogarthian revelry when buying wine in a back-street pub, or explaining that visits to a seedy local revue theatre that specialised in displays of artistic nudity were prompted by the Sickertian quality of the stage lighting. Again, Roger was to be seen at an end-of-term students' party with an unconvincing moustache, dressed as a waiter out of Toulouse-Lautrec.

Members of Roger's generation had their lives disrupted at a time when many were just leaving University. After the war a somewhat naive gaiety and youthful enthusiasm coloured the outlook of many of us who were, half unconsciously, seeking to resume a lost world of normality.

Though the direction of the Painting School was set by Lawrence Gowing, the main task of teaching fell to Christopher Cornford (like

The Open Window (Flavia at Eldon Place), exhibited in the Festival of Britain exhibition, Sixty Paintings for 51 (destroyed)

Lawrence Gowing, 1990

Roger, to depart later to the Royal College) and Roger himself, whose engaging air of informality and patent commitment to the processes and art of painting made him a very effective teacher; even setting out a still-life of bottles, he could make the injunction to paint the space between the bottles, rather than the objects themselves.

The prevailing spirit and character of the Painting School was much influenced by the Euston Road outlook. William Coldstream and Claude Rogers were external examiners, and Sickert occupied a particular eminence of esteem. Among foreign painters, artists such as Vuillard and Braque were admired, but, above all others, Cézanne.

Throughout his career Lawrence Gowing was drawn to the study of a wide variety of artists: Hogarth, Cézanne, Matisse, Bacon, and in 1950 he was finishing his book on Vermeer. Newcastle, though a great city, was not, in the 1950s, much concerned with contemporary art. The municipal art gallery was devoted exclusively to English painting of the more conventional type. However, in post-war Arts Council England it was possible to have access to major Old Master paintings through travelling exhibitions. Newcastle, in the period after 1950 was fortunate in this respect, and this, one feels, contributed to a certain stability and concern for established values in Roger's later development; though never conventional, he was to remain a traditionalist.

In 1950 the City Gallery had a loan exhibition of pictures from Woburn which included the ravishing Gainsborough *Landscape with the Woodcutter and Milkmaid*, while in 1951 the Department organised an exhibition in the University Gallery of pictures from Northumbrian collections, for which Roger often accompanied Lawrence Gowing on forays into the country to choose works. Among the loans from Alnwick was an extraordinary Giulio Romano design for a ceiling, from the Allendale collection came the superb Claude *Baptism of the Eunuch* and the Jan Steen *The Effects of Intemperance*, now in the National Gallery; from Blagdon a Cuyp, and most remarkably, from the Swinburne Collection the *Head of Christ the King*, generally accepted as the work of Jan van Eyck. This exceptional occasion was followed in the University Gallery in 1950-51 by an exhibition of the Ellesmere set of *The Seven Sacraments* by Poussin, an artist whose rigorous style was, of course, particularly congenial to admirers of Cézanne.

Royal College of Art

COLIN HAYES

I had been teaching at the Royal College for about three years when Roger de Grey arrived in 1953. He was beginning to make his name as a painter and I thought very highly of his work.

The painting department was large when I started work because so many of the students had returned from military service simultaneously. Most were already in their late twenties and some were older than I was. One, I remember, was a Major. All worked very hard and assumed they were at the College to learn something. But later on teaching became more difficult when students arrived thinking they already knew rather a lot.

One of Roger's teaching aids, which I helped him set up, was what

Roger de Grey: *Studio Interior* showing
Colin Hayes and a model reflected in a mirror
in the RCA schools, *c*. 1960–65

he called a 'reflective still-life room'. It consisted of mirrors set at angles to each other and a variety of objects placed more or less at random between them. Its purpose was to encourage students to consider the nature of pictorial design. Roger also helped students not so much to copy great paintings as to make transcriptions of them. The point of this was to understand the problems the Masters had to cope with and relate their solutions to students' own work. Roger was very much involved with group tutorials which were also something of an innovation.

Robin Darwin was the Rector and he thought that teachers should do their own work at the College while always being available to talk to the students. The Professor of Painting, Rodrigo Moynihan, had a studio there, and I shared another with Roger. We often painted together – portraits and figure compositions.

I'm not entirely sure why Roger left the College but he did once tell me that he felt he'd been 'second-in-command for long enough'. Roger had been an advisor to the City and Guilds School for some time, and I think an informal approach had already been made. We also suspected that the College painting department was about to change radically. Carel Weight, who had succeeded Rodrigo Monyihan as Professor, was set for retirement in 1974 and Peter de Francia, already teaching part-time, was about to take over.

I believe that Roger's development as a painter was nothing less than heroic. The central concern of his work always remained the same and he never lost sight of it. For him, visual experience had to be reinvented in thoroughly formalised terms, transcribed into an abstract language which worked both in depth and on the flat. But I also think that Roger's painting developed and improved after a difficult middle period. He did not become a different artist, just an increasingly better one.

City and Guilds School

IAN TREGARTHEN JENKIN

Roger de Grey in the City and Guilds School

Roger was a truly marvellous Principal of the City and Guilds School. He put the School on the map and made it stand for something serious. I believe that it became a unique place for the training of artists and craftsmen in this country. He regarded drawing and the fine arts in general as the cornerstones of everything, whether three-dimensional design, restoration or conservation. The notion of the artist-craftsman was crucial to his philosophy.

He was deeply interested in the students, their welfare and progress. Students there received much more close, personal attention than is usual today. They still do. A tremendous amount of teaching went on. Roger always insisted that the teachers were practising artists. In consequence the School had a thoroughly professional atmosphere and was a wonderfully vital place to be. Roger was determined that students should have knowledge of history as well. They were encouraged to go to museums, galleries and current exhibitions, to make full use of everything that London offers. He built up the library substantially, too, beginning almost from nothing.

Roger's ideas and personality galvanised the School and his rare abilities as a fund-raiser put it on a sound financial footing. He raised an enormous amount of money with the aid of that special ability of his to persuade all sorts of people – the livery companies, businesses, private individuals – to do precisely what he wanted. He was one of the last principals of the old school: a practising artist who knew what it was all about and was committed to teaching.

Royal Academy

PIERS RODGERS

Any account of Roger de Grey as President of the Royal Academy is bound to be a personal thing, especially when written by one who was as close to him as I was. And if it has taken us a hundred years to form a dispassionate view of Frederic Leighton's achievements it may be rather too soon to draw a line under Roger's presidency.

Roger never let the dignity of the office overcome his natural gaiety and high spirits, but those superficial characteristics – and the sheer fun of working with him – should not be allowed to obscure the seriousness of his purpose and the passion with which he pursued it.

Of course he had the advantage of a good apprenticeship: nine years as Treasurer during Sir Hugh Casson's presidency. That was when the foundations were laid for a remarkable renascence of the institution; and when in 1984 Sir Hugh retired, Roger was the natural choice to follow him. The survival kit was already in place: the Friends and the RA Trust were founded, sponsorship was pioneered, fees and commissions were introduced; a lively and varied exhibition programme was the motor which drove the Academy forward. As Treasurer, he could take the credit for much of this, but Roger in 1984 had none of the public profile of Hugh Casson. How would he follow that act?

He had had time enough to reflect on the question and at the first Assembly he presided over he declared to a small band of artists in overcoats and hats, with glasses of whisky to hand (it was snowing outside and the heating had broken down) that he wished to involve them more in the running of the institution, and to do more to promote the work of living artists. He knew that the strength of the Membership was the strength of the institution; and he used every means available to bring distinguished artists into it, whether by electing them (sometimes attracting a rebuff, which he always took in good part), by coopting them as Senior Members, inviting them to exhibit, organising shows of their work (in the old Diploma and the new Sackler Galleries, and latterly in the Friends' Room) and generally by making them feel welcome in the Academy. Truly, the Academy became once more an 'Artists' House'.

In defence of art and artists, he was indefatigable. At that first Assembly, he invited one of the students to address the Members on the short-sightedness of the cuts inflicted by the Government on the art schools. It was typical that he wished to give the students a voice and that he should start a debate on a matter of general concern for artists, even though the issue had no direct relevance to the RA (where there was nothing to cut). It was Roger's fervent belief that the Academy should speak for all artists.

Later, he was to suggest interrupting the sequence of the Summer

The Selection Committee for the Summer Exhibition at the Royal Academy 1988.
l-r: Frederick Gore, Leonard McComb, Anthony Eyton, Roger de Grey, Olwyn Bowey

shows for just one year in favour of an exhibition of Members' work – this revolutionary idea never took root among the Members themselves, but it expressed his confidence in them, rather than any lack of concern for others. His efforts to encourage distinguished foreign artists (many of them Honorary Academicians) to send to the Exhibition were also inspired by the belief that the regular exhibitors would come well out of the comparison.

His monument is the Sackler Galleries. Roger's enthusiasm convinced so many, including the Sacklers themselves, to support the project, and his insistence on creating something new in architecture led to the appointment of Foster Associates as architects. It gave him endless satisfaction. Considering he had no head for heights, it was wonderful to see him bounding up the ladders through a maze of scaffolding to inspect progress, often with a terrified 'prospect' in tow. How fitting that his own work should hang in these Galleries.

In architecture 'God is in the details': it was a maxim he applied to everyday life at the Academy. Whether it was the choice of a colour to hang an exhibition on, or his own socks, or a menu or a flower arrangement, Roger wanted it to be 'just so'. His sense of style and attention to detail were present in everything. He and Flavia were memorable upholders of an Academic tradition of conviviality; but if the tradition called for silver candlesticks and good claret, Roger added to it a sense of occasion – of theatre – which was his own. Who will forget the dinner when rose-petals rained down on the heads of the guests?

Roger's affability masked an iron resolve. Though his manner was unfailingly courteous and good-humoured, his exasperation with philistines and his indignation in the face of injustice or discourtesy were formidable. He had a natural reserve which he overcame with difficulty. Each year in December, he persuaded himself that he would be re-elected by the narrowest margin, if at all, and when the result – which was always close to unanimity – was reported to him his sense of relief was palpable.

I have said nothing of Roger's commitment to the Schools, of his unswerving support for the exhibitions, of the tireless work he did to promote art outside the Academy; in short, of the public face of his work. The key to his success as President was that he somehow managed to remain an artist: Friday, Saturday and Sunday were set aside for painting and the last Council meeting of the year would be held earlier and earlier in July, to enable him to get away to his beloved Aquitaine. It was one of the most fertile and productive periods of his life. I doubt that he could have done it without an extraordinary gift of self-discipline, or without the constant support of Flavia, encouraging, supporting, gently chiding, and herself an artist of great distinction.

The Academicians span, by the dates of their election, a period of nearly fifty years. Like a great ship the Academy changes direction slowly although a careless hand on the tiller can cause some alarming gyrations. Roger de Grey's hand was light but firm, and the lasting effects of his Presidency will be seen in years to come.

1 Allotments
1947

'I have gained a great deal of respect for capturing you for the Leicester Galleries . . . the allotments are *distilled*, pure, beautiful. I envy you the beauty of that flying crow terribly; I can't tell you how bright, new, clear and delicious these two pictures looked in London . . .'. (*letter from Lawrence Gowing, 4 April 1948*)

2 Allotments
(Jesmond Dene, Newcastle)
c. 1948

3 Eldon Place
Newcastle upon Tyne:
Autumn
c. 1950

4 Street in Newcastle
c. 1950

5 Eldon Place
c. 1950

6 South Field, Camer
c. 1950

7 Camer Street
c. 1950

10 Interior, Newcastle
c. 1954

8 Eleanor 1951

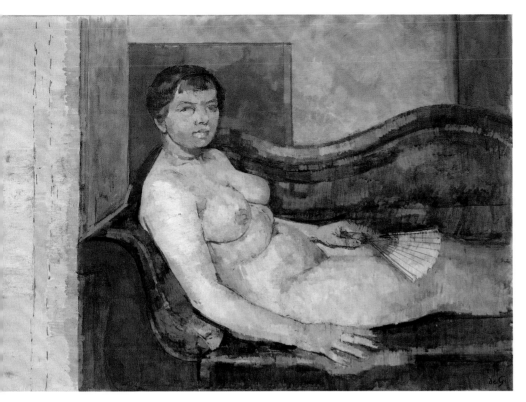

11 Girl with a Fan c.1954

'A painting I did and exhibited
with the London Group got abused
by John Berger who said it was *la
vie bohème*. Anything less, now I've
seen it again, is hard to imagine . . .
the girl . . . is holding a fan in one
hand which I suppose was what he
meant by *la vie bohème* . . . (In
Newcastle) we did used to paint
side by side, Lawrence (Gowing)
and I and Christopher Cornford
sometimes, and my friend Eric
Dobson, in the studios with the
students, and it was a studio pose
in all probability, and the only
privilege that I had was to push
people out of the way and put my
easel where I wanted it'.
(Lambirth, p.150)

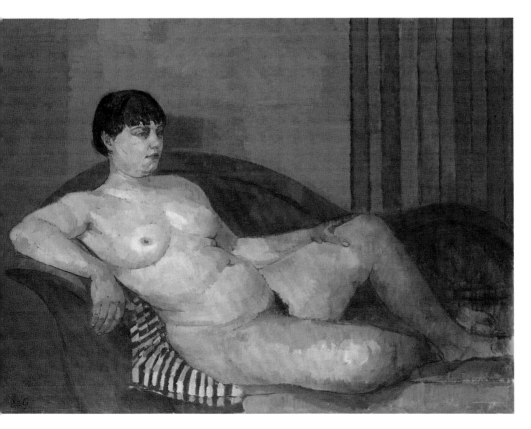

9 Reclining Nude 1950s

13 The Gasometer, Long Benton c.1954

2 Wrotham Hill 1953

14 The Watch House, Seatown *c.* 1956

5 Horton-cum-Studley
, 1954

6 Hell Farm, Dorset,
with Quarry Hill 1955

17 Terraces above Le Rouret *c.* 1959

18 Camer: The Orchard 1959

19 Sole Street, July *c.* 1959

0 The 10.16 from Victoria c. 1959

21 Terrain à Vendre
c. 1959

22 Castagniers
c. 1959

23 March Landscape c. 1960

24 Landscape from the Balcony 1963

5 Le Rouret *c.* 1964

26 Orchard, Meopham
c. 1966

7 The Garden Opposite
1966

28 Little Buckland I
c. 1966

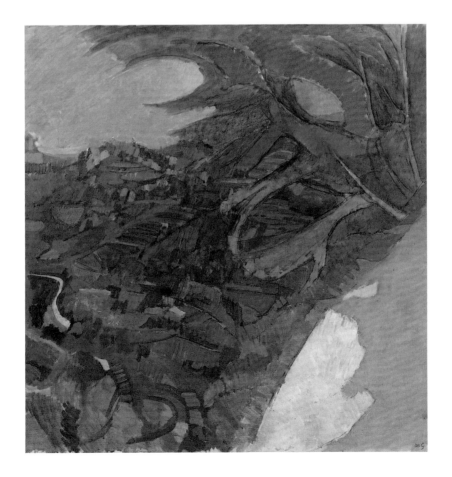

29 Contre Jour II
c. 1966

30 Orchard (Park in Wood) c. 1979

Home

SPENCER DE GREY

Roger and Spencer de Grey,
Christmas Day 1952

It is not possible to talk about Roger without mention of the family. The family was consulted and involved in everything that he did. Gossip was out – debate was in. But the discussions were always light-hearted, sitting out on the terrace in Kent devouring one of his elegantly arranged salads or trying to keep the pither stove roaring in the depths of winter. For the last forty years of his life he and Flavia lived in Kent. Everything was focused on Kent unless they were away on holiday in France.

France in the late fifties and sixties was a farmhouse near Grasse where we spent long, idyllic holidays with Greville and Patricia Poke and their family. Greville was Chairman of the English Stage Company – heated debates about the latest play at the Royal Court or the state of painting at the Royal College continued long into the night. Before departing for France each year, Roger and Greville spent a hectic month designing and producing the annual production for the Old Stagers, one of England's oldest amateur drama companies. The garden was adorned with great canvases of Veronese, effortlessly reproduced by Roger. More recently, France took the form of a house on the edge of the *marais* in the Charente Maritime. Here Roger, when not painting or lying on the beach, could indulge in two of his other great passions – gardening and *bricolage*.

Wherever we were, conversation soon turned to the family, with news of Emilia's most recent concert, Robert's latest building at Milton Keynes or Flavia's exhibition about to open. Roger was fascinated by architecture – one of his projects, a major environmental scheme for the local village, developed with Gale Sieveking, was given an extensive review by the architectural correspondent of *The Observer*. The Sackler Galleries at the Royal Academy were the culmination of this life-long interest. But it was Flavia who was his greatest passion. They were hardly ever apart. Never bored by each other's company, they created an extraordinary partnership.

Roger de Grey and Flavia Irwin in their studio

31 Interior/Exterior c. 1979

2 Interior/Exterior 1977

38 Interior/Exterior
c. 1986

39 Interior/Exterior ▷
1987-8

43 Interior/Exterior 1990

40 Interior/Exterior 1987-8

47 Interior/Exterior
(with Dead Swan) 1993

'We found it on the Thames marshes, its head cut off on an electric wire.
It was rotten and disgusting, but we brought it back. I became obsessed by it'.
(*interview with Richard Cork, The Times, 21 April 1994*)

46 Interior/Exterior c. 1993

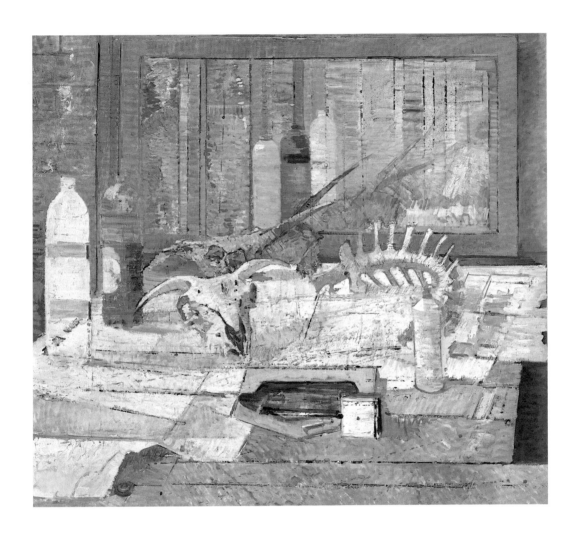

49 Interior/Exterior
(with Skull and Bottles)
1994

48 Interior/Exterior
(with Horse's Skull
and Cockburn's Port)
1994

'I had found an idyll in a particular bit of wood which it seemed would
last the rest of my life'. The wood was south of Bordeaux in St Symphorien,
where the tall trees and dense undergrowth made a closed-in
chamber of colour and filtered light. When de Grey returned the
following summer the wood had been bulldozed flat . . . Not until the
following year did he find another woodland to take its place'.
(Paddy Kitchen, 'Coming to Terms', Country Life, 29 May 1986, p.1541)

33 The Road to St Symphorien, I
1982

'The first marks on the canvas are normally thin washes of colour which aim to recreate the colour sensations extracted from the subject. These non-explicit marks I try to retain for as long as I am able to resist the demands of reality which begin to emerge as opaque paint in the lighter tone range. The process of marrying opaque and limpid paint, substance and shadow, continues throughout the painting. The addition of the textual complexity of nature takes place in the studio'.
(*Roger de Grey, typescript of 26 January 1983 in the de Grey archive*)

35 La Tremblade *c.* 1985

41 La Tremblade 1989

42 Camer Street 1990

37 La Tremblade c.1990

36 Marennes I 1985

45 Marennes 1992-3

44 Marennes Canal: Morning 1990

50 St Just *c.* 1994

51 Marennes *c.* 1994

53 Marennes 1994

52 Exterior (Wall) 1993

54 Bien Assis c. 1994

'I'm tremendously excited about this organisation of the landscape. It's painted in a sort of heat haze. This is a tremendously hot part of France. The landscape is perfectly flat as far as the eye can see . . . This used to be sea and it was reclaimed in the Middle Ages and there's just this great escarpment with a castle on top and you stand there and this whole panorama is laid out like a carpet in front of you'.
(*Roger de Grey in 'Artists and the Landscape', Radio 3, 21 February 1994*)

56 Broue 1994

55 Broue c. 1994

57 Marennes 1994

67 Marennes c. 1993

60 Orchard 1980s

59 Orchard 1980s ▷

61 Rainham *c.* 1986

62 Camer Street 1980s

4 Caen (Sketch 3) *c.* 1992

68 Marennes 1994

63 Les Landes 1985

65 Giudecca Notebook 2, February 1992

66 Marennes *c.*1993

58 Royan 1980s

69 La Tremblade c. 1994

Paintings

1 *Allotments*
1947
43.2 × 74 cm
Arts Council Collection,
Hayward Gallery, London

2 *Allotments*
(Jesmond Dene, Newcastle)
purchased 1948
50.8 × 61.6 cm
Tullie House, City Museum
and Art Gallery, Carlisle

3 *Eldon Place, Newcastle upon Tyne:*
Autumn
exhibited Agnew's, 1950
76 × 101.5 cm
Government Art Collection

4 *Street in Newcastle*
c. 1950
29.5 × 50 cm
Dr and Mrs Andrew Verney

5 *Eldon Place*
c. 1950
49 × 75.1 cm
The Senior Common Room,
University of Newcastle

6 *South Field, Camer*
c. 1950
35 × 51 cm
Private Collection

7 *Camer Street*
c. 1950
60 × 50 cm
Private Collection

8 *Eleanor (Portrait of Eleanor*
Renton on a chaise longue)
1951; exhibited Agnew's,
1954, no. 18;
bought by Clive Bell
62 × 75 cm
The Charleston Trust

9 *Reclining Nude*
1950s
90 × 122 cm
Private Collection, England

10 *Interior, Newcastle*
exhibited Agnew's 1954, no. 5
62.5 × 75.3 cm
Marianne Ford

11 *Girl with a Fan*
exhibited Agnew's, 1954, no. 13
77 × 106 cm
Royal Academy of Arts, London

12 *Wrotham Hill*
1953; exhibited Agnew's,
1954, no. 2
61 × 77.5 cm
Tate Gallery, London
presented by the Trustees
of the Chantrey Bequest

13 *The Gasometer, Long Benton*
exhibited Agnew's 1954, no. 7
63.5 × 76.7 cm
Manchester City Art Galleries

14 *The Watch House, Seatown*
exhibited London Group,
1956, no. 169
63.6 × 101.5 cm
Bought by the late
Mortimer Wilmot Bennitt,
lent by Pamela Galton

15 *Horton-cum-Studley*
exhibited Agnew's, 1954,
no. 24; purchased 1955
64.5 × 76.5 cm
Tullie House, City Museum
and Art Gallery, Carlisle

16 *Hell Farm, Dorset,*
with Quarry Hill
1955
64 × 76 cm
Private Collection, England

17 *Terraces above Le Rouret*
exhibited Agnew's, 1959, no. 43
71 × 91.4 cm
Professor and Mrs Quentin Bell

18 *Camer: The Orchard*
1959
60.9 × 76.2 cm
Private Collection

19 *Sole Street, July*
exhibited Agnew's, 1959, no. 47
71.1 × 91.4 cm
Private Collection

20 *The 10.16 from Victoria*
exhibited Agnew's, 1959, no. 16
63 × 75 cm
Private Collection

21 *Terrain à Vendre*
exhibited Agnew's, 1959, no. 46
50.8 × 63.5 cm
Private Collection

22 *Castagniers*
exhibited Royal Academy
Summer Exhibition and
Agnew's, 1959, no. 13
71 × 92 cm
Royal Academy of Arts, London

23 *March Landscape*
purchased 1960
71.2 × 91.7 cm
Lent by Her Majesty The Queen

24 *Landscape from the Balcony*
1963
71.1 × 91.4 cm
Tate Gallery, London
presented by the Trustees
of the Chantrey Bequest

25 *Le Rouret*
c. 1964
73.6 × 60.9 cm
Tim and Emilia Crawford

26 Orchard, Meopham
exhibited Leicester Galleries,
1966, no. 3
121.9 × 152.4 cm
Arts Council Collection,
Hayward Gallery, London

27 The Garden Opposite
exhibited Nottingham
University Art Gallery,
1966, no. 41
121 × 92.1 cm
The Senior Common Room,
University of Newcastle

28 Little Buckland I
exhibited Leicester Galleries,
1966, no. 17; purchased 1967
63.5 × 76.3 cm
Tullie House, City Museum
and Art Gallery, Carlisle

29 Contre Jour II
exhibited Leicester Galleries,
1966, no. 9
101.6 × 101.6 cm
Arts Council Collection,
Hayward Gallery, London

30 Orchard (Park in Wood)
exhibited Bury St Edmunds,
1979, no 3
149.8 × 101.6 cm
Collection Royal College of Art,
London

31 Interior / Exterior
exhibited Bury St Edmunds,
1979, no. 2
152 × 183 cm
Private Collection

32 Interior / Exterior
1977
182.9 × 88.9 cm
Tate Gallery, London
presented by the Trustees
of the Chantrey Bequest

33 The Road to St Symphorien, I
1982
125 × 90 cm
Private Collection

34 The Road to St Symphorien, II
1982
125 × 90 cm
Private Collection

35 La Tremblade
exhibited Royal Academy
Summer Exhibition, 1985
127 × 91.5 cm
Sir Anthony and Lady Wheeler

36 Marennes I
1985
99 × 120 cm
Prince and Princess von Preussen

37 La Tremblade
c. 1990
105 × 128 cm
Ms Sima Rastegar

38 Interior / Exterior
purchased 1986
151 × 91 cm
Government Art Collection
(inv. no. GAC 16562)

39 Interior / Exterior
1987–8; purchased 1988
122 × 91.5 cm
Government Art Collection
(inv. no. GAC 16638)

40 Interior / Exterior
1987–8
183 × 101 cm
Private Collection

41 La Tremblade
1989
126 × 100 cm
Private Collection

42 Camer Street
1990
105 × 105 cm
Private Collection, England

43 Interior / Exterior
1990
126 × 126 cm
Royal West of England
Academy, Bristol

44 Marennes Canal: Morning
1990
exhibited Royal Academy
Summer Exhibition 1991
147 × 127 cm
Mrs Hana Rayner

45 Marennes
1992–3
exhibited Royal Academy
Summer Exhibition, 1995
101.6 × 121.9 cm
Private Collection, England

46 Interior / Exterior
exhibited Friends Room,
Royal Academy, 1993, no. 5
Diploma work, accepted 1994
137 × 182 cm
Royal Academy of Arts,
London

47 Interior / Exterior
(with Dead Swan)
1993, exhibited Grosvenor
Galleries, 1994, no. 11
101.6 × 101.6 cm
Private Collection, England

48 Interior / Exterior
(with Horse's Skull and
Cockburn's Port)
1994
102 × 102 cm
Private Collection, England

49 Interior / Exterior
(with Skull and Bottles)
1994
91.4 × 101.6 cm
Private Collection, Engla

50 St Just
exhibited Grosvenor
Galleries, 1994, no. 4
101.5 × 101.5 cm
Private Collection, Engla

51 Marennes
exhibited Grosvenor
Galleries, 1994, no. 1
61 × 56 cm
Private Collection

52 Exterior (Wall)
1993
101.6 × 101.6 cm
Private Collection, Engla

53 Marennes
1994
127 × 101.6 cm
Private Collection, Engla

54 Bien Assis
exhibited Grosvenor
Galleries, 1994, no. 5
122 × 127 cm
Private Collection

55 Broue
exhibited Grosvenor
Galleries, 1994, no. 8
127 × 101.5 cm
Private Collection

56 Broue
1994
125 × 94 cm
The Worshipful Compar
Painter-Stainers

57 Marennes
1994
91.4 × 91.4 cm
Private Collection, Engla

Works on paper

8 Royan
1980s
chalk on paper, 36 × 57 cm
Private Collection, England

9 Orchard
1980s
charcoal, 71 × 64.8 cm
Lent by Her Majesty The Queen

0 Orchard
1980s
pencil on paper, 60 × 50.5 cm
Private Collection, England

1 Rainham
1986
brown chalk on paper
0.5 × 50.8 cm
Royal Academy of Arts, London

62 Camer Street
1980s
charcoal on paper
39 × 40.5 cm
Private Collection

63 Les Landes
1985
drawing, 26 × 18.5 cm
Prince and Princess von Preussen

64 Caen (Sketch 3)
acquired 1992
conté, 36.5 × 52 cm
Private Collection

65 Giudecca Notebook 2
February 1992
pastel and chalk on paper
38 × 35.5 cm
Private Collection, England

66 Marennes
c.1993
conté, 49.5 × 35.5 cm
Private Collection

67 Marennes
c.1993
colour conté, 50 × 41 cm
Private Collection, England

68 Marennes
1994
pen and ink on paper,
27.5 × 40 cm
Anna and Charles Utley

69 La Tremblade
exhibited Grosvenor
Galleries, 1994, no. 26
charcoal on paper, 50 × 70 cm
Private Collection

Friends of the Royal Academy

SPONSORS

Mrs Denise Adeane
Mr M.R. Anderson
Mr and Mrs Theodore
  Angelopoulos
Mr P.F.J. Bennett
Mrs D. Berger
Mr David Berman
Mr and Mrs George Bloch
Mrs J. Brice
Mr Jeremy Brown
Mrs Susan Burns
Mr and Mrs P.H.G. Cadbury
Mrs L. Cantor
Mr Christopher Cates
Mrs Denise Cohen
Mrs Elizabeth Corob
Mr and Mrs S. Fein
Mr M. J. Fitzgerald (Occidental
  International Oil Inc.)
Mr and Mrs R. Gapper
Mr and Mrs Robert Gavron
Mr and Mrs Michael Godbee
Lady Gosling
Lady Grant
Mr Harold Joels
Mrs G. Jungels-Winkler
Mr J. Kirkman
Dr Abraham Marcus
The Oakmoor Trust
Ocean Group p.l.c. (P.H. Holt
  Trust)
Mr and Mrs Godfrey Pilkington
Mr and Mrs G.A. Pitt-Rivers
The Worshipful Company of
  Saddlers
Mr and Mrs David Shalit
Mrs Roama Spears
The Stanley Foundation
Mr Helmut Sternberg
Mrs Paula Swift
Mr Robin Symes
Mrs Edna S. Weiss
Mrs Linda M. Williams
Sir Brian Wolfson

ASSOCIATE SPONSORS

Mr Richard B. Allan
Mr Richard Alston
Mr Ian F.C. Anstruther
Mrs Ann Appelbe
Mr John R. Asprey
Lady Attenborough
Mr J.M. Bartos
Mrs Susan Besser
Mrs Linda Blackstone
Mrs C.W.T. Blackwell
Mr Peter Boizot
C.T. Bowring (Charities Trust) Ltd
Mrs J.M. Bracegirdle
Mr Cornelius Broere
Lady Brown
Mr P.J. Brown Jr
Mr T.M. Bullman
Mr and Mrs James Burt
Mrs A. Cadbury
Mr and Mrs R. Cadbury
Mrs C.A. Cain
Miss E.M. Cassin

Mr R.A. Cernis
Mr. S. Chapman
Mr W.J. Chapman
Mrs J.V. Clarke
Mr John Cleese
Mrs R. Cohen
Mrs N.S. Conrad
Mr and Mrs David Cooke
Mr C. Cotton
Mrs Saeda H. Dalloul
Mr and Mrs D. de Laszlo
Mr John Denham
The Marquess of Douro
Mr D.P. Duncan
Mr Kenneth Edwards
Mrs K.W. Feesey MSc
Dr G.-R. Flick
Mr J.G. Fogel
Mr Graham Gauld
Mr Stephen A. Geiger
Mrs R.H. Goddard
Mrs P. Goldsmith
Mr Gavin Graham
Mr and Mrs R.W. Gregson-Brown
Mrs O. Grogan
Mr J.A. Hadjipateras
Mr B.R.H. Hall
Mr and Mrs Richard Harris
Miss Julia Hazandras
Mr Malcolm Herring
Mrs. P. Heseltine
Mrs K.S. Hill
Mr R.J. Hoare
Mr Reginald Hoe
Mr Charles Howard
Mrs A. Howitt
Mr Norman J. Hyams
Mr David Hyman
Mrs Manya Igel
Mr C.J. Ingram
Mr S. Isern-Feliu
The Rt. Hon. The Countess of
  Iveagh
Mrs I. Jackson
Lady Jacobs
Mr and Mrs S.D. Kahan
Mr and Mrs J. Kessler
Mr D.H. Killick
Mr P.W. Kininmonth
Mrs L. Kosta
Mrs E. Landau
Mr and Mrs M.J. Langer
Mrs J.H. Lavender
Mr and Mrs Andrew D. Law
Mr Morris Leigh
Mr J.R.A. Leighton
Mr Owen Luder
Mrs G.M.S. McIntosh
Mr Peter I. McMean
Mrs Susan Maddocks
Ms R. Marek
The Hon. Simon Marks
Mr and Mrs V.J. Marmion
Mr B.P. Marsh
Mr and Mrs J.B.H. Martin
Mr R.C. Martin
Mr and Mrs G. Mathieson
Mr J. Menasakanian
Mr J. Moores
Mrs A. Morgan
Mr A.H.J. Muir
Mr David H. Nelson
Mrs E.M. Oppenheim-Sandelson
Mr Brian R. Oury
Mrs J. Palmer
Mrs J. Pappworth

Mr J.H. Pattisson
Mrs M.C.S. Philip
Mrs Anne Phillips
Mr Ralph Picken
Mr G.B. Pincus
Mr W. Plapinger
Mrs J. Rich
Mr Clive and Mrs Sylvia Richards
Mr F.P. Robinson
Mr M. Robinson
Mr D. Rocklin
Mrs A. Rodman
Lady Rootes
Mr and Mrs O. Roux
The Hon. Sir Stephen Runciman
  CH
Sir Robert Sainsbury
Mr G. Salmanowitz
Mr Anthony Salz
Lady Samuel
Mrs Bernard L. Schwartz
Mr Mark Shelmerdine
Mrs Emma Shulman
Mr R.J. Simmons
Mr John H.M. Sims
Dr and Mrs M.L. Slotover
The Spencer Wills Trust
Mr and Mrs J.G. Studholme
Mr J.A. Tackaberry
Mr N. Tarling
Mr G.C.A. Thom
Mrs Andrew Trollope
Mr A.J. Vines
Mrs C.H. Walton
Mr D.R. Walton Masters
Mr Neil Warren
Miss J. Waterous
Mrs Roger Waters
Mrs J.M. Weingarten
Mrs C. Weldon
Mr Frank S. Wenstrom
Mr Julyan Wickham
Mrs I. Wolstenholme
Mr W.M. Wood
Mr R.M. Woodhouse
Mr and Mrs F.S. Worms

Royal Academy Trust

BENEFACTORS

H.M. The Queen
Mr and Mrs Russell B. Aitken
American Airlines
The Annie Laurie Aitken Charitable
  Trust
American Associates of the Royal
  Academy Trust
American Express Company
Mrs John W. Anderson II
The Andor Family
The Hon. and Mrs Walter H.
  Annenberg
Mr Walter Archibald
Marilyn B. Arison
The Hon. Anne and Mr Tobin
  Armstrong
Asprey
AT & T
AT & T (UK) Ltd
Barclays Bank plc
Mr and Mrs Sid R. Bass

Mr Tom Bendhem
Benihana Group
Mrs Brenda Benwell-Lejeune
Mr David Berman
In Memoriam: Ida Rose Biggs
Charlotte Bonham-Carter
  Charitable Trust
Denise and Francis Booth
British Airways, North America
British Gas plc
The British Petroleum
  Company plc
BP America
British Steel plc
Mr Keith Bromley
The Brown Foundation Inc.
BT
BUNZL plc
Iris and B. Gerald Cantor
Sir Richard Carew Pole
The Rt. Hon. the Lord Carrington
The Trustees of the Clore
  Foundation
The Cohen Family Charitable Trust
The John S. Cohen Foundation
The Ernest Cook Trust
Mrs John A. Cook
Crabtree & Evelyn
The Hon. and Mrs C. Douglas
  Dillon
Sir Harry and Lady Djanogly
In Memoriam: Miss W.A. Donner
The Dulverton Trust
Alfred Dunhill Limited
Miss Jayne Edwardes
The John Ellerman Foundation
Mr E.A. Emerson
English Heritage
The Eranda Foundation
The Esmée Fairbairn Charitable
  Trust
Esso UK PLC
Lord and Lady Faringdon
Mr and Mrs Eugene V. Fife
Mr and Mrs Donald R. Findlay
Mr Walter Fitch III
Mrs Henry Ford II
The Henry Ford II Fund
The Foundation for Sport and
  the Arts
The Late John Frye Bourne
The Garfield Weston Foundation
Gartmore plc
The Gatsby Foundation
The Getty Grant Program
The J. Paul Getty Jr Trust
The Lady Gibson
Glaxo Wellcome plc
The Jack Goldhill Charitable Trust
Maurice and Laurence Goldman
The Horace W. Goldsmith
  Foundation
The Worshipful Company of
  Goldsmiths
The Greentree Foundation
The Worshipful Company of
  Grocers
The Worshipful Company of
  Haberdashers
The Paul Hamlyn Foundation
The Late Dr and Mrs Armand
  Hammer
Mrs Sue Hammerson
Philip and Pauline Harris
  Charitable Trust
Mr and Mrs Gustave Hauser

The Hayward Foundation
Mr and Mrs Randolph Hearst
Klaus and Belinda Hebben
The Hedley Foundation
Mrs Henry J. Heinz II
The Henry J. and Drue Heinz
  Foundation
Drue Heinz Trust
The Heritage of London Trust
The Howser Foundation
The Idlewild Trust
The J.P. Jacobs Charitable Trust
Jerwood Foundation
Mr and Mrs Donald P. Kahn
The Kresge Foundation
The Kress Foundation
Mr and Mrs Sol Kroll
Ladbroke Group Plc
Mr D.E. Laing
The Kirby Laing Foundation
The Maurice Laing Foundation
  Fund
The Landmark Hotel
The Landmark Trust
The Lankelly Foundation
Mr John S. Latsis
The Leche Trust
The Leverhulme Trust
Mr Leon Levy and Ms Shelby White
Lex Service Plc
The Linbury Trust
The Ruth and Stuart Lipton
  Charitable Trust
Sir Sydney and Lady Lipworth
Mr John Madejski
Mrs T.S. Mallinson
The Manifold Trust
The Stella and Alexander Margulies
  Charitable Trust
Mr and Mrs John L. Marion
Marks & Spencer
Mrs Jack C. Massey
M.J. Meehan & Company
Mr. Paul Mellon KBE
The Anthony and Elizabeth
  Mellows Charitable Trust
The Mercers' Company
Mr and Mrs Donald Moore
The Henry Moore Foundation
Museums and Galleries
  Improvement Fund
National Westminster Bank PLC
Diane A. Nixon
The Normanby Charitable Trust
Otemae College
The Peacock Charitable Trust
Mr and Mrs Frank Pearl
The Pennycress Trust
In Memoriam: Mrs Olive Petit
The P.F. Charitable Trust
The Pilgrim Trust
Mr A.N. Polhill
The Hon. and Mrs Leon B. Polsky
Provident Financial plc
The Radcliffe Trust
The Rayne Foundation
Mr and Mrs Laurance S.
  Rockefeller
The Ronson Charitable Foundation
Mr and Mrs Leonard Rosoman
Rothmans UK Holdings Limited
The J. Rothschild Group Charitable
  Trust
Rothschilds Inc
Royal Mail International
The RTZ - CRA Group

The Late Dr Arthur M. Sackler
Mrs Arthur M. Sackler
The Sainsbury Family Charitable
  Trusts
Mrs Jean Sainsbury
Mrs Basil Samuel
Save & Prosper Educational Trust
Mrs Frances G. Scaife
Sea Containers Limited
Sheeran Lock
Shell UK Ltd
The Archie Sherman Charitable
  Trust
Mr and Mrs James C. Slaughter
The Late Mr Robert Slaughter
Pauline Denyer Smith and Paul
  Smith CBE
Sotheby's
The Spencer Charitable Trust
Miss K. Stalnaker
The Starr Foundation
The Steel Foundation
Bernard Sunley Charitable
  Foundation
Lady Judith Swire
Mr and Mrs A. Alfred Taubman
Mr and Mrs Vernon Taylor Jr.
Texaco Inc
Time Out Magazine
G. Ware and Edythe Travelstead
Seiji Tsutsumi
The Douglas Turner Charitable
  Trust
The 29th May 1961 Charitable
  Trust
Unilever PLC
The Weldon UK Charitable Trust
Mr and Mrs Keith S. Wellin
The Welton Foundation
Westminster City Council
Mr and Mrs Garry H. Weston
The Hon. and Mrs John C.
  Whitehead
Mrs John Hay Whitney
Mr Frederick B. Whittemore
Mr and Mrs Wallace S. Wilson
The Wolfson Foundation
The Late Mr Charles Wollaston
The Late Mr Ian Woodner
Mr and Mrs William Wood Prince

Corporate Membership Scheme

Sponsors of Past Exhibitions

The Council of the Royal
Academy thanks sponsors
of past exhibitions for their
support. Sponsors of major
exhibitions during the last
ten years have included the
following:

Alitalia
Italian Art in the 20th Century
1989

Allied Trust Bank
Africa: The Art of a Continent
1995

American Express Foundation
Je suis le cahier: The Sketchbooks
of Picasso 1986

**Anglo American Corporation of
South Africa**
Africa: The Art of a Continent
1995

The Banque Indosuez Group
Pissarro: The Impressionist and
the City 1993

Banque Indosuez and W.I. Carr
Gauguin and The School of Pont-
Aven: Prints and Paintings 1989

BBC Radio One
The Pop Art Show 1991

BMW (GB) Limited
Georges Rouault: The Early Years,
1903-1920 1993
David Hockney: A Drawing
Retrospective 1995

Bovis Construction Ltd
New Architecture 1986

British Airways
Africa: The Art of a Continent
1995

British Alcan Aluminium
Sir Alfred Gilbert 1986

British Petroleum Company plc
British Art in the 20th Century
1987

BT
Hokusai 1991

Canary Wharf Development
New Architecture 1986

Cantor Fitzgerald
From Manet to Gauguin:
Masterpieces from Swiss Private
Collections 1995

The Capital Group Companies
Drawings from the J. Paul Getty
Museum 1993

The Chase Manhattan Bank
Cézanne: the Early Years 1988

Chilstone Garden Ornaments
The Palladian Revival: Lord
Burlington and his House and
Garden at Chiswick 1995

Christie's
Frederic Leighton 1830-1896
1996

Classic FM
Goya: Truth and Fantasy, The Small
Paintings 1994
The Glory of Venice: Art in the
Eighteenth Century 1994

**The Dai-Ichi Kangyo Bank
Limited**
222nd Summer Exhibition 1990

The Daily Telegraph
American Art in the 20th Century
1993

De Beers
Africa: The Art of a Continent
1995

Deutsche Morgan Grenfell
Africa: The Art of a Continent
1995

Digital Equipment Corporation
Monet in the '90s: The Series
Paintings 1990

The Drue Heinz Trust
The Palladian Revival: Lord
Burlington and his House and
Garden at Chiswick 1995

The Dupont Company
American Art in the 20th Century
1993

The Economist
Inigo Jones Architect 1989

Edwardian Hotels
The Edwardians and After:
Paintings and Sculpture from the
Royal Academy's Collection,
1900-1950 1990

Electricity Council
New Architecture 1986

Elf
Alfred Sisley 1992

Esso Petroleum Company Ltd
220th Summer Exhibition 1988

Fiat
Italian Art in the 20th Century
1989

Financial Times
Inigo Jones Architect 1989

Fondation Elf
Alfred Sisley 1992

Ford Motor Company Limited
The Fauve Landscape: Matisse,
Derain, Braque and their Circle
1991

Friends of the Royal Academy
Sir Alfred Gilbert 1986

Gamlestaden
Royal Treasures of Sweden, 1550-
1700 1989

Joseph Gartner
New Architecture 1986

**J. Paul Getty Jr Charitable
Trust**
The Age of Chivalry 1987

Glaxo Wellcome plc
From Byzantium to El Greco 1987
Great Impressionist and other
  Master Paintings from the Emil
  G. Bührle Collection, Zurich
  1991
The Unknown Modigliani 1994

The Guardian
The Unknown Modigliani 1994

Guinness plc
Twentieth-Century Modern
  Masters: The Jacques and
  Natasha Gelman Collection 1990
223rd Summer Exhibition 1991
224th Summer Exhibition 1992
225th Summer Exhibition 1993
226th Summer Exhibition 1994
227th Summer Exhibition 1995
228th summer exhibition 1996

Guinness Peat Aviation
Alexander Calder 1992

Harpers & Queen
Georges Rouault: The Early Years,
  1903-1920 1993
Sandra Blow 1994
David Hockney: A Drawing
  Retrospective 1995

The Henry Moore Foundation
Henry Moore 1988
Alexander Calder 1992
Africa: The Art of a Continent
  1995

The Independent
The Art of Photography 1839-
  1989 1989
The Pop Art Show 1991

**Industrial Bank of Japan,
  Limited**
Hokusai 1991

Intercraft Designs Limited
Inigo Jones Architect 1989

**Joannou & Paraske-Vaides
  (Overseas) Ltd**
From Byzantium to El Greco
  1987

The Kleinwort Benson Group
Inigo Jones Architect 1989

Lloyds Bank
The Age of Chivalry 1987

Logica
The Art of Photography, 1839-
  1989 1989

The Mail on Sunday
Royal Academy Summer Season
  1992
Royal Academy Summer Season
  1993

Marks & Spencer
Royal Academy Schools
  Premiums 1994
Royal Academy Schools Final Year
  Show 1994

Martini & Rossi Ltd
The Great Age of British
  Watercolours, 1750-1880
  1993

Paul Mellon KBE
The Great Age of British
  Watercolours, 1750-1880 1993

Mercury Communications
The Pop Art Show 1991

Merrill Lynch
American Art in the 20th
  Century 1993

Midland Bank plc
The Art of Photography 1839-
  1989 1989
RA Outreach Programme 1992-
  1996
Lessons in Life 1994

Minorco
Africa: The Art of a Continent
  1995

**Mitsubishi Estate Company UK
  Limited**
Sir Christopher Wren and the
  Making of St Paul's 1991

Mobil
From Byzantium to El Greco
  1987

Natwest Group
Reynolds 1986
Nicolas Poussin 1594-1665
  1995

Olivetti
Andrea Mantegna 1992

Otis Elevators
New Architecture 1986

**Park Tower Realty
  Corporation**
Sir Christopher Wren and the
  Making of St Paul's 1991

Pearson plc
Eduardo Paolozzi Underground
  1986

Pilkington Glass
New Architecture 1986

Redab (UK) Ltd
Wisdom and Compassion: The
  Sacred Art of Tibet 1992

Reed International plc
Toulouse-Lautrec: The Graphic
  Works 1988
Sir Christopher Wren and the
  Making of St Paul's 1991

**Republic National Bank of
  New York**
Sickert: Paintings 1992

The Royal Bank of Scotland
Royal Academy Schools Final Year
  Show 1996

Arthur N. Sackler Foundation
Jewels of the Ancients 1987

Salomon Brothers
Henry Moore 1988

The Sara Lee Foundation
Odilon Redon: Dreams and
  Visions 1995

Sea Containers Ltd.
The Glory of Venice: Art in the
  Eighteenth Century 1994

Silhouette Eyewear
Egon Schiele and His
  Contemporaries: From the
  Leopold Collection, Vienna 1990
Wisdom and Compassion: The
  Sacred Art of Tibet 1992
Sandra Blow 1994
Africa: The Art of a Continent
  1995

Société Générale, UK
Gustave Caillebotte: The
  Unknown Impressionist
  1996

Société Générale de Belgique
Impressionism to Symbolism: The
  Belgian Avant-Garde 1880-1900
  1994

Spero Communications
The Royal Academy Schools Final
  Year Show 1992

Texaco
Selections from the Royal
  Academy's Private Collection
  1991

The Times
Old Master Paintings from the
  Thyssen-Bornemisza Collection
  1988
Wisdom and Compassion: The
  Sacred Art of Tibet 1992
Drawings from the J. Paul Getty
  Museum 1993
Goya: Truth and Fantasy, The Small
  Paintings 1994
Africa: The Art of a Continent
  1995

Tractebel
Impressionism to Symbolism: The
  Belgian Avant-Garde 1880-1900
  1994

Unilever
Frans Hals 1990

Union Minière
Impressionism to Symbolism: The
  Belgian Avant-Garde 1880-1900
  1994

Vistech International Ltd
Wisdom and Compassion: The
  Sacred Art of Tibet 1992

Other Sponsors

Sponsors of events, publications
and other items in the past two
years:

Academy Group Limited
Agnew's
Air Hong Kong
Air Jamaica
Air UK
Alitalia
Allied Trust Bank
Arthur Andersen
John A. Anderson
Athenaeum Hotel and
  Apartments
Austrian Airlines
Mr and Mrs Martin Beisly
The Beit Trust
Berggruen & Zevi Limited
The Britto Foundation
The Brown Foundation
Bulgari Jewellery
James Butler RA
Cable & Wireless
The Calouste Gulbenkian
  Foundation (Lisbon)
Cathay Pacific
Chilstone Garden Ornaments
Christopher Wood Gallery
Citibank N.A.
Terance Cole
Columbus Communications
Condé Nast Publications
Shimona Cowan
Deutsche Morgan Grenfell
Hamish Dewar
Jennifer Dickson RA
The Elephant Trust
Brenda Evans
Sebastian de Ferranti
Fina Plc
FORBES Magazine, New York
Forte Plc
The Four Seasons Hotels
Isabel Goldsmith
Ivor Gordon
Lady Gosling
Julian Hartnoll
Ken Howard RA
IBM UK Limited
Inter-Continental Hotels
Intercraft Designs Limited
Jaguar Cars Limited
John Lewis Partnership plc
A.T. Kearney Limited
KLM
Count and Countess Labia
The Leading Hotels of the World
The Leger Galleries, London
The A.G. Leventis Foundation
Mr and Mrs J.H.J. Lewis
The Maas Gallery
Mandarin Oriental Hotel Group
Martini & Rossi Ltd
Masterpiece
Mercury Communications Ltd
Merrill Lynch
NK
The Nigerian Friends of africa95
Novell U.K. Ltd
Richard Ormond
Patagonia
Penshurst Press Ltd

Mr and Mrs James Phelps
Stuart Pivar
Polaroid (UK) Ltd
Price Waterhouse
The Private Bank & Trust
  Company Limited
Ralph Lauren
The Regent Hotel
The Robina Group
The Rockefeller Foundation
N. Roditi & Co.
Royal Mail International
Mrs Basil Samuel
Sears Plc
Simon Dickinson Ltd
Peyton Skipwith
Swan Hellenic Ltd
Mr and Ms Daniel Unger
Kurt Unger
Vista Bay Club Seychelles
Vorwerk Carpets Limited
John Ward RA
Warner Bros.
W. S. Yeates plc
Mrs George Zakhem
ZFL